I0788174

Notebook

Pretty Blue Notebook to Write,
Journal and Take Notes in.

Hardcover ISBN: 978-1-989733-06-6
Published in December 2019
Lined Journal

This book belongs to:

____

9 781989 733066